My United States
Florida

WITHDRAWN

TAMRA B. ORR

Children's Press®
An Imprint of Scholastic Inc.

Content Consultant
James Wolfinger, PhD, Associate Dean and Professor
College of Education, DePaul University, Chicago, Illinois

Library of Congress Cataloging-in-Publication Data
Names: Orr, Tamra, author.
Title: Florida / by Tamra B. Orr.
Description: New York, NY : Children's Press, 2017. | Series: A true book | Includes bibliographical references and index.
Identifiers: LCCN 2017002076 | ISBN 9780531252543 (library binding) | ISBN 9780531232842 (pbk.)
Subjects: LCSH: Florida—Juvenile literature.
Classification: LCC F311.3 .O77 2017 | DDC 975.9—dc23
LC record available at https://lccn.loc.gov/2017002076

Photographs ©: cover: Roger Ressmeyer/Corbis/VCG/Getty Images; back cover ribbon: AliceLiddelle/Getty Images; back cover bottom: klikk/iStockphoto; 3 bottom: Ian Dagnall/Alamy Images; 3 map: Jim McMahon; 4 bottom: Steven David Miller/Minden Pictures; 4 top: PjrStudio/Alamy Images; 5 top: Fotoluminate LLC/Shutterstock; 5 bottom: Anna Kucherova/Shutterstock; 6 inset: Pete Titmuss/Alamy Images; 7 bottom: FloridaStock/Shutterstock; 7 top: Linda Moon/Shutterstock; 7 center: Ian Dagnall/Alamy Images; 8-9: franckreporter/iStockphoto; 11: GALA Images/Alamy Images; 12: Pat Canova/Alamy Images; 13: Win McNamee/Getty Images; 14: Fotoluminate LLC/Shutterstock; 15 center: blickwinkel/Alamy Images; 15 top: Zoonar/S.Foote/age fotostock; 15 bottom: Pacific Stock - Design Pics/Superstock, Inc.; 16-17: traveler1116/iStockphoto; 19: Bill Cotterell/AP Images; 20: Tigatelu/Dreamstime; 22 left: Atlaspix/Shutterstock; 22 right: Steve Allen/Shutterstock; 23 center left: mlorenz/Shutterstock; 23 center right: José Lucas/age fotostock/Superstock, Inc.; 23 bottom left: Anna Kucherova/Shutterstock; 23 bottom right: Media Bakery; 23 top left: PjrStudio/Alamy Images; 23 top right: Valery Voennyy/Alamy Images; 24-25: Sarin Images/The Granger Collection; 27 left: Werner Forman/TopFoto/The Image Works; 27 right: Theodore Morris; 29: North Wind Picture Archives/Alamy Images; 30: Fonollosa/Iberfoto/The Image Works; 31 left: Everett Collection Historical/Alamy Images; 31 right: Science & Society Picture Library/Getty Images; 31 center: Atlaspix/Shutterstock; 32: Science & Society Picture Library/Getty Images; 33: Bettmann/Getty Images; 34-35: Gavin Hellier/Alamy Images; 36: Jonathan Ferrey/Getty Images; 37: Hannes Gritzke/Alamy Images; 38: US Navy Photo/Alamy Images; 39: Matt Stroshane/Getty Images; 40 inset: HannLeonPhoto/iStockphoto; 40 bottom: PepitoPhotos/iStockphoto; 41: age fotostock/Superstock, Inc.; 42 top left: Chronicle/Alamy Images; 42 top right: Universal Images Group North America LLC/Alamy Images; 42 center left: Earl Theisen Collection/Getty Images; 42 center right: Bettmann/Getty Images; 42 bottom: PA Images/Alamy Images; 43 top right: ZUMA Press/Alamy Images; 43 top left: AF archive/Alamy Images; 43 center left: Robert Galbraith/REUTERS/Alamy Images; 43 bottom left: Harry Langdon/Getty Images; 43 bottom center: William Thomas Cain/Getty Images; 43 center right: David Livingston/Getty Images; 43 bottom right: PA Images/Alamy Images; 44 top: Peter Ptschelinzew/Getty Images; 44 bottom right: NAN728/Shutterstock; 44 bottom left: Doug Perrine/Minden Pictures; 44 center: Anna Kucherova/Shutterstock; 45 top: Paolo Marchesi/Aurora; 45 center: gorosan/Shutterstock; 45 bottom: Pete Titmuss/Alamy Images.

Maps by Map Hero, Inc.

All rights reserved. Published in 2018 by Children's Press, an imprint of Scholastic Inc.
Printed in the United States of America 113

**Front cover: Space shuttle *Discovery*
launching from Kennedy Space Center**

**Back cover: Cypress trees growing
in a swamp**

Welcome to Florida

UNITED STATES

Florida

Find the Truth!

Everything you are about to read is true **except** for one of the sentences on this page.

Which one is **TRUE**?

T or F No part of Florida is more than 60 miles (97 km) away from the coast.

T or F The first people ever to live in Florida were Spanish explorers.

Find the answers in this book.

3

Contents

THE **BIG** TRUTH!

Horse
conch

What Represents Florida?

American alligator

4

Palm trees in Miami

Florida
orange juice

This Is Florida!

ALABAMA

GEORGIA

ATLANTIC OCEAN

Florida Panhandle

State Capitol

★ **TALLAHASSEE**

PENSACOLA

Gulf Islands National Seashore

JACKSONVILLE

FLORIDA

St. Augustine

Daytona International Speedway

UNIVERSAL

OCALA

Universal Orlando

2

John F. Kennedy Space Center

N
W E
S

GULF OF MEXICO

Plant City

Florida Peninsula

ORLANDO

3

Walt Disney World/ EPCOT/ MGM Studios

TAMPA

ST. PETERSBURG

PLANT CITY

Bok Tower

The John and Mable Ringling Museum of Art

SARASOTA

WEST PALM BEACH

The Villa Vizcaya Museum and Gardens

Sanibel Island

4

MIAMI

Everglades National Park

Miami Beach

KEY WEST
Florida Keys

0   50
Miles

1 Gulf Islands National Seashore

Glistening white beaches, historic landmarks, and marshes teeming with life are just a few of the attractions within this protected place.

② Kennedy Space Center

Since the 1960s, the Kennedy Space Center has been the launching point of many of America's space missions. Visitors can tour the facility and learn more about the history of U.S. space exploration.

③ Walt Disney World

One of the world's most popular vacation destinations, Walt Disney World covers 43 square miles (111 square kilometers) near Orlando and contains several theme parks, water parks, hotels, and more.

④ Everglades National Park

This unique national park is one the country's most important wilderness areas. Established to protect Florida's wetlands, it is home to many rare plants and animals.

BAHAMAS

More than 15.5 million people visit the Miami area and its beaches each year!

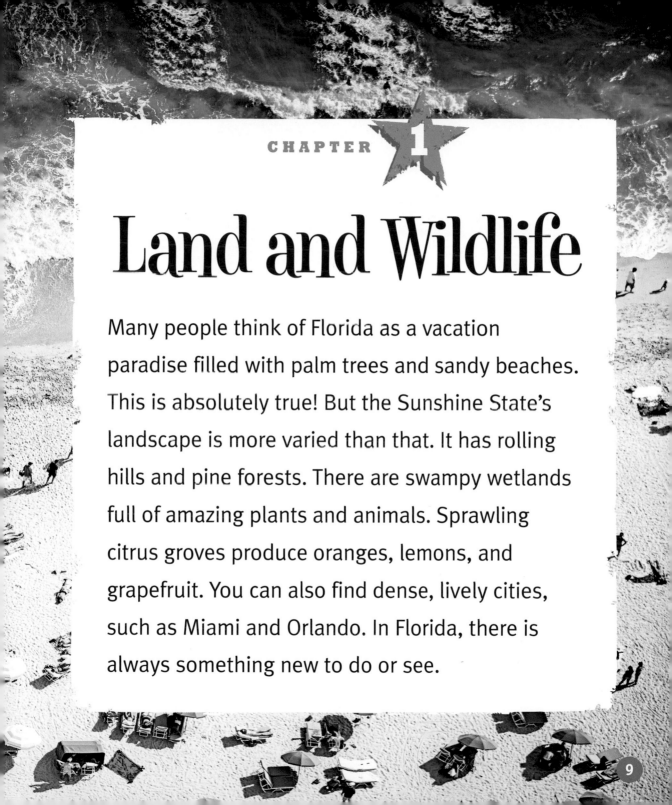

CHAPTER 1

Land and Wildlife

Many people think of Florida as a vacation paradise filled with palm trees and sandy beaches. This is absolutely true! But the Sunshine State's landscape is more varied than that. It has rolling hills and pine forests. There are swampy wetlands full of amazing plants and animals. Sprawling citrus groves produce oranges, lemons, and grapefruit. You can also find dense, lively cities, such as Miami and Orlando. In Florida, there is always something new to do or see.

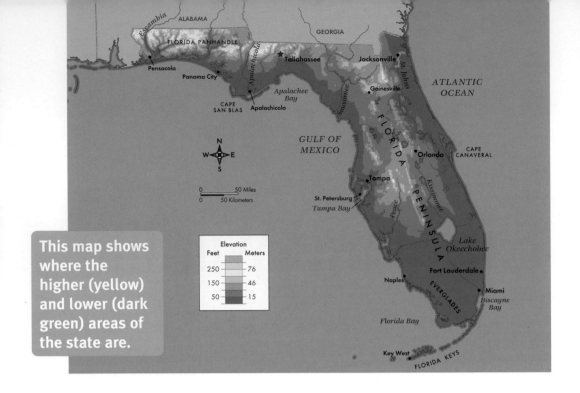

This map shows where the higher (yellow) and lower (dark green) areas of the state are.

Beaches Everywhere

Florida sticks out of the southeastern corner of the United States like a handle. While the top of the state borders Georgia and Alabama, most of Florida is a **peninsula**. It is surrounded on all three sides by water—the Atlantic Ocean and the Gulf of Mexico. As a result, the state has about 1,350 miles (2,173 km) of coastline. No single point in Florida is more than 60 miles (97 km) from a coastline!

The Florida Keys

Just off the coast of south Florida is a chain of small islands called the Florida Keys. The keys stretch for about 150 miles (241 km). They are linked to the mainland by the Overseas Highway. It has 42 bridges—the longest is the 6.7-mile-long (10.8 km) Seven Mile Bridge. The name *keys* comes from the Spanish word *cayos*, meaning "small islands."

No Mountains Here

Florida is one of the country's flattest states. The only hills you'll find are in the northern part of the state, along its border with Georgia.

Sinkholes are found throughout much of Florida. Some of them are so large they have been turned into lakes, biking trails, and even tourist attractions.

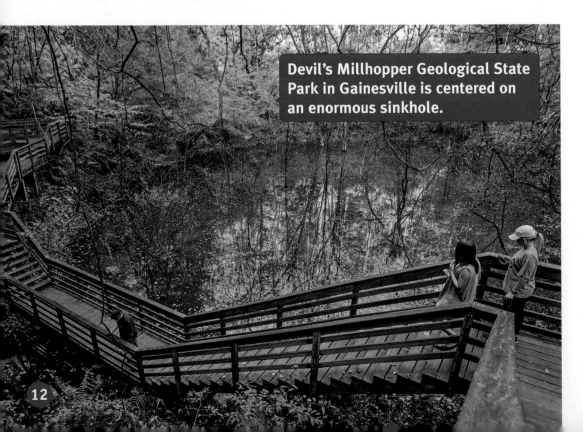

Devil's Millhopper Geological State Park in Gainesville is centered on an enormous sinkhole.

MAXIMUM TEMPERATURE
109°F

MINIMUM TEMPERATURE
-2°F

Hurricanes and other storms often cause flooding in Florida's towns and cities.

Climate

When cold winter weather hits the rest of the country, many people begin packing their bags for a trip to Florida. They may come for a few days, weeks, or even months. They soak up as much sunshine and warmth as possible. The state has a subtropical **climate**. This means it never gets very cold. Florida does get some rough weather. Fierce tropical storms and **hurricanes** can strike the state, usually between June and November.

Florida's palm trees can grow to be more than 60 feet (18.3 meters) tall.

Palms, Pines, and Oranges

Palm trees are a well-known symbol of Florida. More than a dozen types grow here, including coconut and date palms. Florida also has about 300 other species of trees, including pines and hardwoods. Fascinating trees like the strangler fig, gumbo-limbo, and mangrove all grow here. Florida's sunny climate is also perfect for growing oranges and other citrus fruits. Gray-green Spanish moss hangs from tree limbs. About 4,000 species of flowering plants add splashes of color everywhere you look.

Florida's Fauna

Nearly 500 native bird species fill Florida's sky, including hawks, eagles, herons, and pelicans. Rivers and lakes are inhabited by alligators, crocodiles, and many types of fish. Turtles, frogs, toads, snakes, and lizards can be spotted throughout the state. The ocean is home to manatees, sharks, dolphins, jellyfish, and whales. Land animals include armadillos, black bears, and Florida panthers. Florida is also known for fire ants, extra-large cockroaches, and other insects.

Great blue heron

Armadillo

Manatees are closely related to elephants.

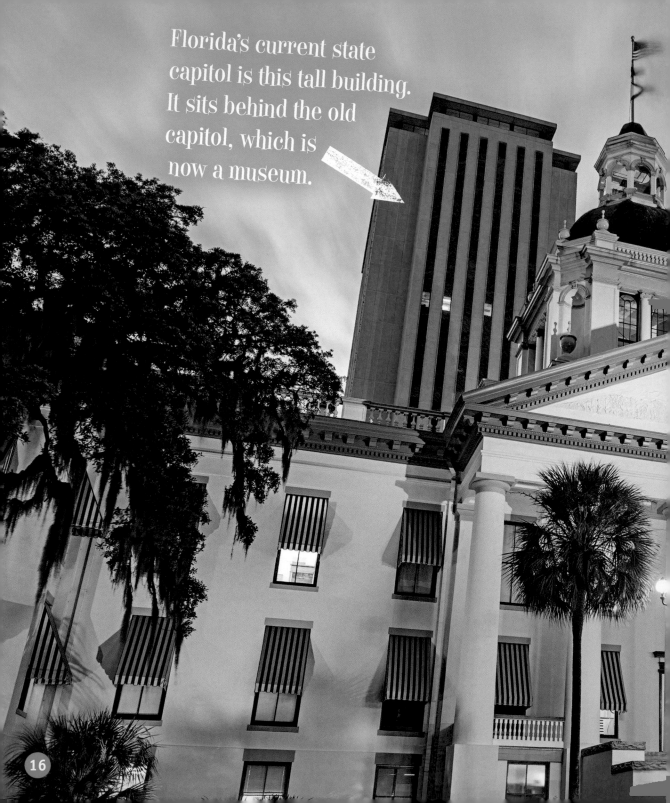

Florida's current state capitol is this tall building. It sits behind the old capitol, which is now a museum.

CHAPTER 2

Government

Since 1824, Tallahassee has served as the capital of Florida. The city is located in the northern part of the state, near the border with Georgia. This is where elected officials meet to discuss new laws and keep the state government running smoothly. Like the U.S. government, Florida's state government is made up of three branches: executive, legislative, and judicial.

State Government Basics

The executive branch is led by the governor. The main job of the executive branch is to carry out laws. The legislative branch focuses on creating laws. It consists of two parts. One is the House of Representatives, which has 120 members. The other is the Senate, which has 40 members. Florida's judicial branch enforces the state's laws. The state courts decide if laws have been broken and what punishment is needed.

FLORIDA STATE GOVERNMENT

LEGISLATIVE BRANCH
Writes and passes state laws

Senate (40 members)	House of Representatives (120 members)

EXECUTIVE BRANCH
Carries out state laws

Governor	Attorney General	Chief Financial Officer	Commissioner of Agriculture

Lt. Governor	Commissioner of Education	Secretary of State

JUDICIAL BRANCH
Enforces state laws

State Supreme Court

District Courts of Appeal (5 divisions)

Circuit Courts (20 divisions)

County Courts (67 divisions)

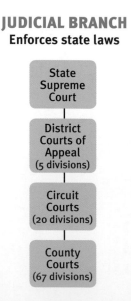

The Florida legislature meets to write new laws and debate changes to existing laws.

Florida's State Constitution

The rules outlining each branch's responsibilities are laid out in Florida's constitution. This document was first written in 1838. Since then, it has gone through a number of changes. The current version was adopted in 1968. Every 20 years, Florida's legislature reviews its constitution to see if it needs any changes, or **amendments**.

Florida's National Role

Every state has members in the U.S. Congress. Each state, including Florida, has two senators. The number of representatives in the House of Representatives depends on a state's population. Florida has 27.

Each state also has a certain number of votes to apply in the election of the U.S. president. These electoral votes are equal to the number of members of Congress. With two senators and 27 representatives, Florida has 29 electoral votes.

2 senators and 27 representatives

29 electoral votes

With 29 electoral votes, Florida has a strong voice in presidential elections.

Representing Florida

Elected officials in Florida represent a population
with a range of interests, lifestyles, and backgrounds.

Ethnicity (2015 estimates)

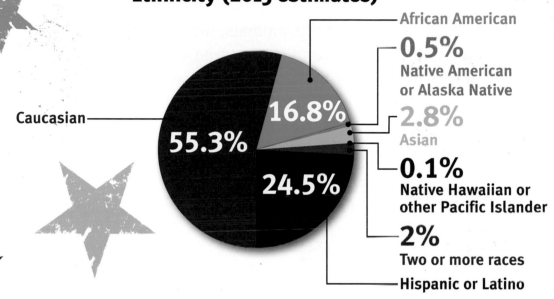

Caucasian

55.3%

16.8% — African American

0.5% Native American or Alaska Native

2.8% Asian

0.1% Native Hawaiian or other Pacific Islander

24.5%

2% Two or more races

Hispanic or Latino

27% of the population have a degree beyond high school.

20% of Floridians were born in other countries.

65% own their own homes.

91% live in cities.

87% of the population graduated from high school.

1/3 speak a language other than English at home.

What Represents Florida?

States choose specific animals, plants, and objects to represent the values and characteristics of the land and its people. Find out why these symbols were chosen to represent Florida or discover surprising curiosities about them.

Seal

Florida's state seal was first created in 1868. Since then, it has been slightly changed a few times. The current state seal combines symbols of Florida's history, industry, and plant life. It pictures a Native American woman, a sabal palm tree, and a steamboat under the rays of the rising sun.

Flag

When Florida's state flag was created in 1868, it featured the state seal on a white background. But during the 1890s, Governor Francis Fleming worried that the flag's all-white background was too similar to the white flag of surrender. So a red cross was added in 1900.

Horse Conch or Giant Band Shell

STATE ANIMAL

Found in the waters near Florida, these shells can be up to 2 feet (0.6 m) long.

Moonstone

STATE GEM

This gemstone is not actually found in Florida. Instead, it was chosen to remind people of Florida's role in space exploration.

Orange Blossom

STATE FLOWER

These flowers grow on the trees that produce Florida's famous oranges.

Florida Panther

STATE ANIMAL

There are only about 160 of these amazing cats left in the wild today, and all of them live in Florida.

Orange Juice

STATE BEVERAGE

With so many oranges growing in Florida's groves, it's no surprise that this juice is a local favorite.

Key Lime Pie

STATE PIE

This sweet treat is made using key limes, which grow throughout the Florida Keys.

23

R.Holata   Outina.

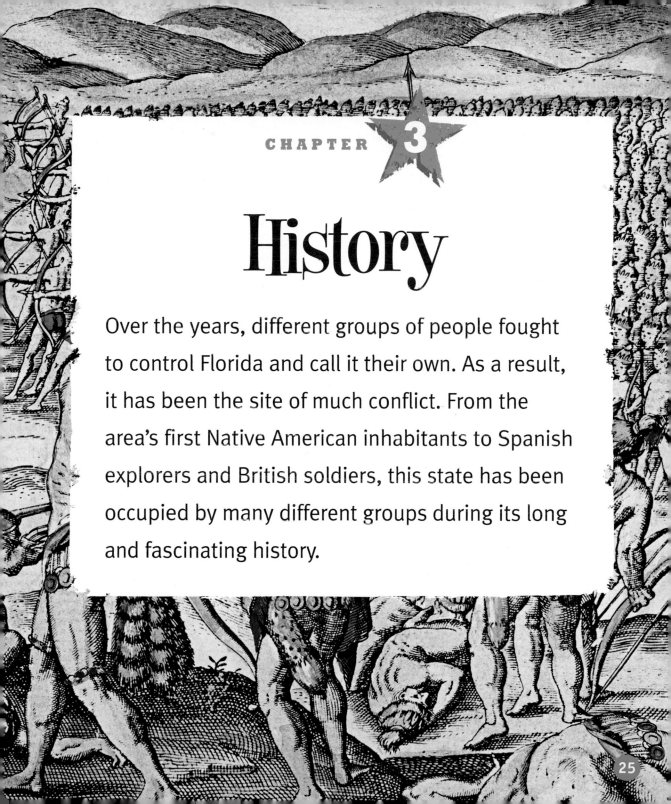

CHAPTER 3

History

Over the years, different groups of people fought to control Florida and call it their own. As a result, it has been the site of much conflict. From the area's first Native American inhabitants to Spanish explorers and British soldiers, this state has been occupied by many different groups during its long and fascinating history.

This map shows the general areas where Native American groups settled.

Native Americans

The very first people who lived in the area now known as Florida arrived more than 12,000 years ago. These hunters and gatherers lived mainly on the small game they caught. They also gathered plants, nuts, and shellfish. They made weapons and tools from stone. Over the years, they began making pottery.

These early people eventually developed into several cultural groups. Among them were the Calusas, the Apalachees, the Tequestas, the Tocobagas, and the Timucuans. Many of Florida's native people were farmers. They planted crops of corn, squash, and beans. Those living near the coast often ate seafood, including fish, turtles, and other aquatic animals. Shells and bones from these animals could also be used to make tools, jewelry, and other items.

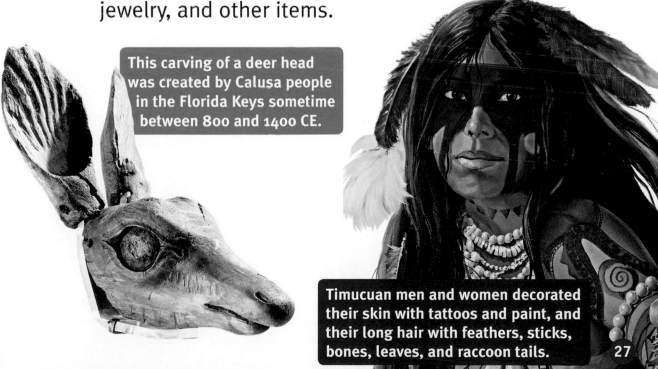

This carving of a deer head was created by Calusa people in the Florida Keys sometime between 800 and 1400 CE.

Timucuan men and women decorated their skin with tattoos and paint, and their long hair with feathers, sticks, bones, leaves, and raccoon tails.

European Exploration

Spanish explorer Juan Ponce de León waded ashore on Florida's coast for the first time in spring 1513. He had come in search of gold and resources for Spain. In honor of the area's many flowers and the time of year—Easter—he named the region Florida. The name is from the Spanish phrase *Pascua Florida*, which means "Flowery Easter."

Other European explorers followed. By 1565, both France and Spain had established settlements in Florida.

This map shows the routes taken by the explorers in the 1500s.

Ponce de León and his men battle Calusa people in 1521.

Spain controlled Florida for nearly 200 years. But following the Seven Years' War (1756–1763), Great Britain took ownership of the region. It remained in control of Florida until the end of the American Revolution (1775–1783), when a peace **treaty** returned ownership of the region to Spain.

Becoming a State

In the 1800s, the United States began claiming parts of Florida. In 1819, Spain agreed to transfer Florida to the United States, which took control in 1821.

Between 1817 and 1858, Native Americans battled the U.S. Army in an effort to keep control of their homeland. They were defeated, and the United States established permanent control of the area. On March 3, 1845, Florida became the 27th U.S. state.

Timeline of Florida Events

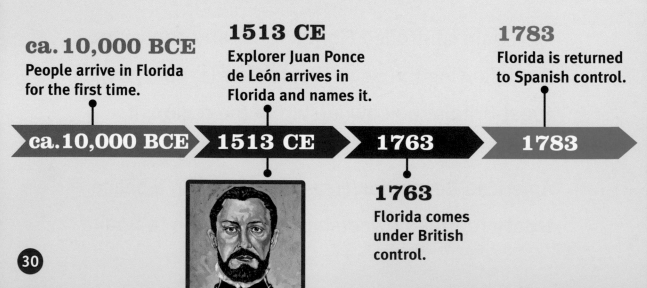

ca. 10,000 BCE
People arrive in Florida for the first time.

1513 CE
Explorer Juan Ponce de León arrives in Florida and names it.

1783
Florida is returned to Spanish control.

ca. 10,000 BCE | 1513 CE | 1763 | 1783

1763
Florida comes under British control.

A Country Divided

In 1861, Florida **seceded** from the Union and joined the other Southern states as part of the **Confederacy**. During the Civil War (1861–1865), the Union defeated the Confederacy. Florida was readmitted to the Union in 1868. Following the war, Florida focused on rebuilding the cities and towns that had been damaged during the war. The state's people also built better roads and train routes.

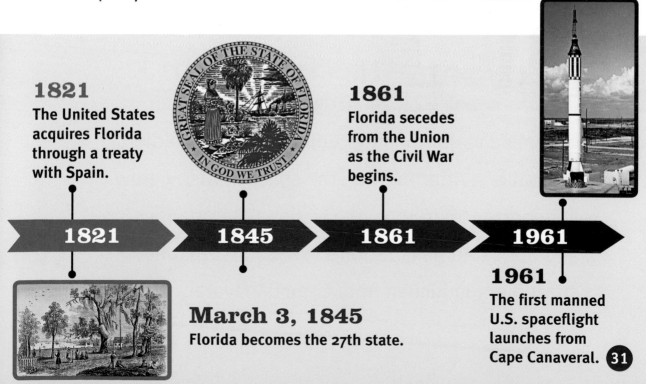

1821
The United States acquires Florida through a treaty with Spain.

1861
Florida secedes from the Union as the Civil War begins.

1821   **1845**   **1861**   **1961**

March 3, 1845
Florida becomes the 27th state.

1961
The first manned U.S. spaceflight launches from Cape Canaveral.

The Mercury-Redstone 3 spacecraft launches from Cape Canaveral on May 5, 1961. It was the first U.S. craft to carry humans into space.

On to Today

In the 20th century, people began to realize that Florida's warm weather and sunny beaches could make it a popular winter vacation spot. Investors all over the country sank money into the state's tourism industry.

During World War II (1939–1945), Florida became a major training center for pilots, soldiers, and sailors. After the war, the space industry grew in importance. In 1961, the National Aeronautics and Space Administration's (NASA) first manned spaceflight launched from Cape Canaveral.

The Father of Florida

Henry Morrison Flagler (1830–1913) was born in New York. However, he is considered the father of Florida. Flagler came to Florida in 1878, after cofounding the Standard Oil Company. He disliked the state's railroad service, so he decided to improve it. Flagler created a train route all the way to Key West. He also built hotels along the way for weary travelers, helping to make Florida a vacation destination.

Miami's Wynwood Art District features street art on over 80,000 square feet (7,432 square meters) of walls.

CHAPTER 4

Culture

What happens when you combine Native American traditions, Spanish history, and southern charm with a healthy dose of Cuban and other Latino influences? You get the people of Florida! The state is a fascinating mix of personalities, ideas, customs, and cultures. This means that Florida is always changing and always exciting!

Florida at Play

Florida is famous for its many golf courses and tennis courts. Because the weather is usually good, people travel from all over to play their favorite sports in the Sunshine State.

If you prefer to watch other people play sports, you'll have plenty of choices in Florida. If you like baseball, you're especially in luck. In addition to the state's home teams, the Miami Marlins and Tampa Bay Rays, many other pro teams head to Florida to hold their annual spring training camps.

Time to Celebrate

You'll never run out of things to do and see in Florida. Take a stroll through Miami's Wynwood Art District to see some of the world's most colorful street art. In St. Petersburg, stop by the Salvador Dali Museum. You can also visit any of Florida's numerous festivals for a day of fun! How about a songwriters' festival, an international science-fiction film festival, a rodeo and parade, or a chili cook-off? You're invited to all of them!

A traditional Cuban band performs in Miami.

At Work

Floridians work in a wide range of fields. It should be no surprise that one of the state's biggest employers is the tourism industry. Many people work at the hotels, restaurants, theme parks, and other attractions that draw so many visitors to Florida. Florida is also a major center of agriculture and technology jobs. For example, many scientists and engineers work at the Kennedy Space Center.

Researchers experiment with protective suits for astronauts at NASA's Kennedy Space Center in Cape Canaveral.

Short-Term Work

With so many businesses centered on agriculture and tourism, Florida is a major source of **seasonal** jobs. These jobs are not long-term careers. Instead, workers are hired for a few weeks or months at a time. For example, an orange grove might hire seasonal workers to help harvest fruit. Also, a hotel might hire extra workers during the busiest times of the year.

Floribbean Food

Eating can be a real adventure in Florida. Southern sweet tea is a favorite drink to go with the Cubano, a sandwich made of pork, ham, Swiss cheese, pickles, and mustard on Cuban bread. Seafood is plentiful, so how about some conch fritters or fried gator tail? Caribbean food in Florida is often called Floribbean and includes oxtail and curried goat. Key lime pie is a popular dessert invented in Florida.

 ## Cubano Sandwiches

Ask an adult to help you!

Ingredients
1/2 stick (1/4 cup) butter, softened
1 loaf Cuban bread, sliced lengthwise
3 tablespoons yellow mustard

1 1/2 pounds ham, sliced
1 1/2 pounds roasted pork, sliced
1 pound Swiss cheese, sliced
1 cup dill pickle chips

Directions
Spread the butter on one half of the bread and the mustard on the other half. Place one or two layers each of the ham, pork, and cheese on the bread, then top with the pickles. Close the sandwich and wrap it tightly in aluminum foil. Press down on the wrapped sandwich to flatten it. Toast the wrapped sandwich in a 350°F oven for 5 to 7 minutes. Unwrap, slice, and serve!

The Sunshine State

Whether you live in Florida or are there on vacation, there's no better place to drink some freshly squeezed orange juice, watch a car race, or collect a few seashells. The Sunshine State is filled with beauty, rich in history, and bathed in year-round warmth and sunlight. ★

More than 50,000 people visit Florida's Walt Disney World theme park every day.

Famous People

Harriet Beecher Stowe

(1811–1896) was a writer who was best known for her novel *Uncle Tom's Cabin*, which was about slavery in the United States. She spent winters in Florida for many years.

Thomas Edison

(1847–1931) was the inventor of the first successful light bulb, the phonograph, and many other devices. He had a laboratory in Fort Myers.

Ernest Hemingway

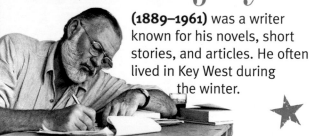

(1889–1961) was a writer known for his novels, short stories, and articles. He often lived in Key West during the winter.

A. Philip Randolph

(1889–1979) was an activist who fought for civil rights and workers' rights. He grew up in Jacksonville.

Sidney Poitier

(1927–) is an actor and filmmaker who made history in 1964 when he became the first African American man to win an Academy Award. He was born in Miami.

Burt Reynolds

(1936–) is an Academy Award–nominated actor who has starred in countless films and TV series. He grew up in Florida and attended Florida State University.

Wallace Amos

(1936–) is the founder of the Famous Amos chocolate chip cookie brand. He was born in Tallahassee.

Janet Reno

(1938–2016) was the first woman to hold the office of attorney general of the United States. She was born and raised in Miami.

William H. Macy

(1950–) is an actor and filmmaker who has appeared in many movies, TV shows, and plays. He was born in Miami.

Ben Vereen

(1946–) is a Tony Award–nominated actor, singer, and dancer who has appeared in many Broadway plays. He was born in Miami.

Bob Vila

(1946–) is known for hosting several popular television programs about home improvement. He was born in Miami.

David Robinson

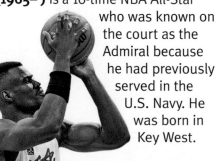

(1965–) is a 10-time NBA All-Star who was known on the court as the Admiral because he had previously served in the U.S. Navy. He was born in Key West.

Did You Know That . . .

Florida is home to three national parks: Biscayne National Park, Dry Tortugas National Park, and Everglades National Park. You can also visit several national memorials, monuments, seashores, and preserves.

In addition to the Florida mainland, the state's boundaries also include about 4,500 islands.

Florida produces more than half of all U.S. oranges. Most Florida oranges are made into juice.

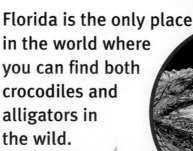

Florida is the only place in the world where you can find both crocodiles and alligators in the wild.

You can find about 7,700 lakes scattered throughout Florida. The largest, Lake Okeechobee, covers 700 square miles (1,813 sq km).

No dinosaur fossils have ever been discovered in Florida. This is because the state was completely underwater during the time dinosaurs roamed the planet.

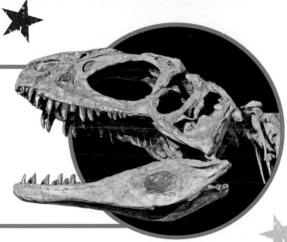

Did you find the truth?

(T) No part of Florida is more than 60 miles (97 km) away from the coast.

(F) The first people ever to live in Florida were Spanish explorers.

Resources

Books

Nonfiction

Orr, Tamra B. *Florida*. New York: Children's Press, 2014.

Suben, Eric. *The Spanish Missions of Florida*. New York: Children's Press, 2010.

Fiction

Blume, Judy. *Starring Sally J. Freedman as Herself*. Scarsdale, NY: Bradbury Press, 1977.

Lenski, Lois. *Strawberry Girl*. New York: J. B. Lippincott Company, 1945.

Rawlings, Marjorie Kinnan. *The Yearling*. New York: C. Scribner's Sons, 1938.

Movies

Apollo 13 (1995)

Armageddon (1998)

Flight of the Navigator (1986)

Flipper (1996)

The Muppet Movie (1979)

Summer Rental (1985)

Visit this Scholastic website for more information on Florida:

 www.factsfornow.scholastic.com
Enter the keyword **Florida**